Dividend Investment

A Simple Guide to Passive Income and Financial Freedom with Dividend Stocks. Retire Early With Smart Investing

Richard James

© **Copyright 2018 - All rights reserved.**

The content contained within this book may not be reproduced, duplicated or transmitted without direct written permission from the author or the publisher.

Under no circumstances will any blame or legal responsibility be held against the publisher, or author, for any damages, reparation, or monetary loss due to the information contained within this book. Either directly or indirectly.

Legal Notice:

This book is copyright protected. This book is only for personal use. You cannot amend, distribute, sell, use, quote or paraphrase any part, or the content within this book, without the consent of the author or publisher.

Disclaimer Notice:

Please note the information contained within this document is for educational and entertainment purposes only. All effort has been executed to present accurate, up to date, and reliable, complete information. No warranties of any kind are declared or implied. Readers acknowledge that the author is not engaging in the rendering of legal, financial, medical or professional advice. The content within this book has been derived from various sources. Please consult a licensed professional before attempting any techniques outlined in this book.

By reading this document, the reader agrees that under no circumstances is the author responsible for any losses, direct or indirect, which are incurred as a result of the use of information contained within this document, including, but not limited to, — errors, omissions, or inaccuracies

Table of Contents

Introduction 7
Don't Put All Your Eggs in One Basket 7
Becoming a Super Investor 9
Why You Need To Invest 9
- Save For Retirement 9
- Earn Higher Income 10
- Reduce Taxable Income 10
- Help Businesses to Grow 11

How Much Money Should You Invest? 11
- Difference between Savings and Investments 11

Questions to Help You Determine How Much You Want To Invest 13
- How much tolerance do I have? 13
- When Do I Need To Access The Money? 13
- Are You Willing To Sacrifice Your Current Standard of Living For Your Dreams? 14

Adopting the Traits of Super Investors 14
- Acquire the right temperament 15
- Learn the ropes! 16
- Understand the risks involved 16
- Understand your investments 17

Understanding the Stock Market 18
Basic Terminologies Used In the Stock Market ... 18
- Shares 18
- Bonds 19
- Equity 19
- Shareholder 20
- Initial Public Offering (IPO) 20
- Earnings per Share 21
- Ticker Symbol 21

    Book Value... 21
    Corporations... 22
What are Stocks?.. 22
    Types of Stocks... 23
Why Do Companies Sell Shares?............................ 24
What is the Stock Market?...................................... 26
    How Does The Stock Market Work?..................... 26
Stock Market Indexes.. 27
Bullish and Bearish Markets................................... 28
Stock Market Corrections and Crash..................... 29
Analyzing the Stock Market.................................... 29
Fundamental Market Analysis................................ 29
    Technical Market Analysis..................................... 30
Why You Need To Diversify..................................... 31
When to Sell Your Stocks.. 32
    Why Selling Is So Hard.. 32
    Wait! Ask Yourself These Questions before Selling Your Shares... 33
Introduction to Dividend Investment........................... 36
What is Dividend Investment?................................ 36
So, How Did It All Start?.. 36
Terms to Know In Dividend Investment................. 38
    Cash Dividends... 38
    Declaration Date... 38
    Dividend Cover Ratio.. 39
    Dividend Reinvestment Plan (DRIP).................... 39
    Dividend Yield... 39
    Record Date... 40
    Ex-dividend Date... 40
    Payment Date.. 40
    One-time Dividends.. 41
Rules of Dividend Investments............................... 41

- Always Go For Quality! 41
- The Bargain Principle 41
- Always Play Safe 42
- Reinvest Your Dividends 42
- Understand Your Tax Laws 42
- Don't Make Dividends Your Only Priority 43
- Watch Out For Value Traps 43
- Always Look Out For Special Dividends 43
- Use the Survival of the Fittest Principle 44

Using Dividends as a Passive Income 45

Misconceptions of Dividend Investment 45
- High Yields Are a Priority 46
- Dividend Stocks are Boring 47
- Financial Flexibility 47
- Organic growth 47
- Dividends are Safe 48
- Dividends Guarantee Downside Protection and Upside Potentials 49

Why Is Dividend Investment So Powerful? 50
Why Do Companies Pay Dividends? 50
- Arguments against Dividends 51
- Arguments for Dividends 52

How Companies Pay Out Dividends 53
- Residual Dividends 53
- Stability Dividends 54
- Hybrid Dividend 55
- Stock Dividends 56
- Property Dividends 57

Snowball Effect; Harnessing the Power of Reinvestment 58

How to Choose Companies to Invest In 59

    Choose Companies that Dominate Their Industries. 59

    Only Invest In Businesses You Understand............... 60

    Don't Limit Your Investments to Two or Three Sectors 60

Harnessing the Power of the Snowball Effect........... 61

How Compound Interest Works...................................... 62

Factors That Influence Compound Rates................... 63

    Interest Rate... 63

    Tax Rate... 64

    Time.. 64

Understanding the Time Value of Money in Compound Interests.. 64

    A Compound Table Showing the Value of $10,000 Invested With Varying Interest Rates.................. 66

Immutable Dividend Strategies.................................... 67

Dogs of the Dow Strategy... 67

    Variations of Dogs of the Dow Strategy..................... 69

    Small Dogs of the Dow... 69

    Dow 4.. 69

    Foolish 4... 69

Dividends Reinvestment Plan (DRIP)........................ 70

Dividend Exchange Traded Funds (ETF)................... 71

The Dividend Capture Strategy..................................... 72

    What is Dividend Capture Strategy?........................... 73

    How It Works... 73

    Real-Life Example... 74

    Shortcomings of Dividend Capture............................. 75

How to Build Your Dividend Portfolio........................... 76

Building a Diversified Global Portfolio....................... 76

    How many investments should you have?................. 77

    Do you really understand your investments?............ 77

    Can you explain why you bought each stock?.......... 78

- Do you still have some investment touched after buying? 78
- Do you frequently add new investments to your portfolio? 79

Robinhood Trading Software as an Effective Tool to Build Your Dividend Portfolio 79
- What You Need To Know Before Investing in Robinhood 80

Mistakes You Ought To Avoid with Robinhood 83
- Never buy in real-time 83
- Add Money In Advance 83
- Don't Check Your Stocks Every Day 84
- Don't Rely on Robinhood For All Your Research! 84

Conclusion 85

Introduction

Our dreams are our driving force. I What makes you wake up every morning and go to work? What makes you study, or work for long hours in order to get that degree or promotion? I'm sure we will arrive at the same answer - our dreams. We dream of a better future, where we get to live life to the fullest. We dream of an early retirement and numerous vacations. We dream of fat bank accounts and changing the lives of our loved ones, and this keeps us awake at night. Yes, dreams are like life jackets thrown out to us in the stormy and uncertain conditions of life. We hold on to these dreams like someone on the verge of drowning, without concern for the time spent or energy expended in chasing it. Sadly, not everyone gets to attain their desired goals. Why? It is because most people tend to rely on just one stream of income to help them achieve their goals. And that, my dear reader, is one of the most dangerous decisions to ever take.

Don't Put All Your Eggs in One Basket

This is an age-old advice that depicts the irreplaceable benefits of having a passive income. Passive income is one of the ways to achieve your financial goals within a shorter time frame. It's a way of earning without spending much effort or energy. In other words, you earn money automatically. Yes, it's that awesome. Passive income removes you from the rat race and offers you more control over your time. Since time is money, it offers you control over finances. Once you have a passive income, you don't have to struggle to meet your monthly financial quota. However, earning a passive income is not an easy feat, as when you start, it requires enormous effort and careful decision making. Earning a passive income requires you to place your "eggs in the right basket," and there's no better niche to invest your income in than dividend investments.

Dividend investment involves earning dividends from your shares in a corporation. Although it's overlooked by many new investors, dividends investments are a sure-fire way of getting passive income. In fact, dividend investments account for a large percentage of stock returns. Mind you, dividend investing is not a get-rich-quick scheme. It requires the ability to understand the financial market and more importantly, to be extremely patient. So, get ready to explore the innumerable benefits and intricacies of dividends. In the following chapters, you will learn the golden rules, strategies and methods you need to excel in this field. Who knows - maybe you might become the next Warren Buffet!

Becoming a Super Investor

Every day, you come across internet ads and brokers promising to make you a "super" investor. You must come across a few of these adverts every week. It's a pity that many jump on this bandwagon of investment without learning how to properly navigate the world of stocks. The word, "investor" has been bandied around so many times that it has lost its value. It is, thereforenot a surprise to see some lose their life fortune all in the name of investment. Investing your money allows you to build wealth. More so, it involves putting your money in areas that have the potential to create huge returns. You really deserve to accomplish your dreams. However, if you are still undecided about investing or not, here are a few reasons to get you on board.

Why You Need To Invest

Here's another question for you: How would you feel on retirement day if your friend or work buddy was sitting on a million-dollar investment, and you weren't? Regret? Pain, Disappointment? These negative emotions will definitely crop up in the future unless you take the necessary steps against this.

Save For Retirement

The government retirement funds just aren't enough to meet your future needs. There is plenty of uncertainty surrounding the future, and it is wise to safeguard it. You can invest your retirement savings into investment portfolios, such as bonds, real estate, stocks, and precious metals. So, you can comfortably live off funds earned from investments when it's time to retire. Here's another angle to this: you can earn a continuous income every month or annually by investing your retirement savings in dividend stocks. You can also re-invest income from dividends into more stocks. Wait! Don't let me spill the beans just yet. I will explain all the principles of dividend investment in the next chapter.

Earn Higher Income

Well, this part is obvious. What's the essence of investing if you can't achieve your financial goals? However, this part is quite tricky as not all stocks are worth investing in. The stock market appreciation can remain stagnant for years. A typical example is the Dow Jones, which remained stagnant for 17 years. The Dow Jones is one of the oldest running US market index. This market index reached 995 in January 1966 and it did not surpass the 995-price level until December 1982. Now, imagine if you had invested in this index. This means your investment portfolio was stagnant for 17 years, with no appreciation at all. Therefore, always invest in stocks that will guarantee a continuous income despite the upheavals of the stock market.

Reduce Taxable Income

This is a win-win situation. First, you get to invest and at the same time, you reduce your taxable income. By putting part of your pre-tax income into an investment plan, you will save more money. In addition to this, if you incur a loss from an investment, you may apply that loss against any profit from other investments, and this lowers the amount of your taxable income.

Help Businesses to Grow

No matter how small you invest, your money can make a huge impact on an ailing business. Investing is about more than just gaining profit, it involves backing new ventures with the potential of creating cutting-edge products. Ultimately, you are building a future for yourself and the businesses you invest in.

How Much Money Should You Invest?

How much should I save and put into my investment portfolio? This question has always been on the lips of new investors. Although it's a straightforward question, its answer has always eluded many. Since there's no clear-cut rule on how much you need to invest, most investors often save or invest lower and this can affect their long-term financial goals. Before we proceed, it is important to know the difference between savings and investments.

Difference between Savings and Investments

Fact is, many investors don't know that savings and investments are two completely different entities, that play different roles, and have different functions. So, before you set out on the journey to building wealth through passive income, you need to understand these concepts.

Savings is the process of storing cold hard cash in an

extremely safe yet liquid account. Liquid, in this context, means that it's stored in a place that allows you to easily access your cash within a short time frame. These include savings accounts supported by the FDIC, checking accounts, and treasury bills. Some savings accounts come with interest rates, but these are usually too small to create a passive income. Many investors including those who lived through the Great Depression recommend keeping a store of cold hard cash in case of a meltdown or market crash.

Investments, on the other hand, is the process of using your capital to procure an asset that you think has a good chance of generating an acceptable income during the course of your investment. You are reading this book to learn how to invest due to the promise of a continuous source of income. You should know that there are many factors that threaten your investment, and a single mistake can wipe out part of your investment portfolio, or even worse, wipe it out in its entirety.

Before you embark on a journey of becoming a super investor, it is necessary to save. Think of savings as a foundation upon which you build your financial structures. You should know that your savings are what provide you with the capital for your investments. Those who don't save are likely to sell off their investments in hard times, and this is not a recipe for getting rich. Therefore, as a general rule, you ought to save an amount that's sufficient to cover all your personal expenses, including your mortgage and utility bills for a span of six months.

Questions to Help You Determine How Much You Want To Invest

First, start by asking yourself these questions, which will help you to arrive at your answer.

How much passive income do I want to earn from my investments? Perhaps you want enough passive income to buy a new house or pay off your mortgage. While trying to arrive at your desired figure, take into account the price of the things you want and the cost of upkeep.

How much tolerance do I have?

In other words, how high is your risk tolerance? Can you tolerate watching your investment value move wildly up and down? The quicker you want to reach your target financial goals, the bigger the fluctuation in your investment value. Sometimes, you may have to watch your accounts go up by 50 percent or go down by 70 percent.

When Do I Need To Access The Money?

This question is vital, especially when you are using tax-deferred accounts like 401[k] or Roth IRA. You can invite heavy penalties and taxes if you withdraw your money from these accounts before the age of 59. Furthermore, you need to calculate the number of years you want to build up your portfolio for in order to increase the compound interest rates.

Are You Willing To Sacrifice Your Current Standard of Living For Your Dreams?

The Answer

Now, let's look at how we can provide an answer to the main question: how much should you invest? I would say that you already have a fair idea of how you want to live in the future. Perhaps, you have picked your dream house, car, or holiday on an exotic island. Or, you have calculated the sufficient amount for your kids' college fees? Now that you have those images in mind, ask yourself this: how much money do I need to achieve this and live the way I want? Would it take $10,000 per year? Perhaps it would take $150,000. Calculate your total income per year and divide it by 0.4 to discover the assets it would require to back that level of annual income. The next thing you need to figure out is how soon you need the money. Let's say you are 30 and you plan to retire by the age of 60. That gives you 30 years of continuous savings. By increasing the amount you save every month, you effectively reduce the number of years needed to reach your financial target. Mind you, do not take this to the extreme. Money solely exists for you to create opportunities for your loved ones and lead a better lifestyle. Don't overdo it!

Adopting the Traits of Super Investors

Successful investors have certain traits in common, irrespective of their investment portfolios. Whether you earn a tidy sum every month from invest incomes and dividends, or you are a financial genius with a laudable portfolio of high investment returns, these traits will ensure that you stay afloat the uncertainties of the financial market.

So, before you jump on to the notion of becoming an investor, you need to adopt certain traits to survive the financial market.

Acquire the right temperament

Yes, having the right temperament can make a lot of difference in the financial world. Mind you, this has nothing to do with discernment, intelligence or wisdom. It simply means developing the right attitude. For instance, patience is a strong trait you need to develop, as you should understand that some things take time. As I mentioned earlier, investing is not a get-rich-quick scheme. Your investment will not magically turn into a huge sum overnight. Heck, you will hardly see the result of your investment in the first few years.

In addition to exercising patience, learn to stay away from the crowd. Yes, you must be willing to stick to a plan while ignoring the will of the crowd. This brings to mind the 1990's dot.com bubble, when some of the world's best investors refused to be swayed by public opinion. These super investors recognized that bubbles don't last. So, you should know that not every stock or asset is worth investing in. Some investors stick to earning dividends, rents, and interest incomes in order to avoid the uncertainties of the stock market.

Lastly, don't get too emotional. In fact, you will hardly reach your financial goal if you are clouded by emotions. Learn to separate market fluctuations from the inherent value of your assets. For example, let's say you bought an apartment building that nets you $100,000 per year in passive income, and someone comes around and offers to buy the building for $200,000 – you would probably laugh in their face since you know the inherent value of the building.

Learn the ropes!

There's no shortcut or cheat to this method. It is vital for you to know how to calculate the intrinsic value of your assets, and this includes getting familiar with the terms, regulations and laws of investment. It doesn't matter if it's a government bond, a share of stock or a car wash business; you will be at a disadvantage if you don't know to pull out a calculator and punch in the figures yourself. Yes, the calculations involved look daunting or impossible. However, don't lose heart. All you have to do is to continually ask yourself this question - "how much do I have to pay for a dollar of net present earnings?" Your net present earning is the difference between the current value of your cash inflow and the current value of your outflows. By asking yourself this question over and over again, you will notice your thoughts becoming clearer. In fact, it will help you to sieve genuine and high returns from shady investments. Remember, it only takes a few good financial decisions to reach your desired target.

Understand the risks involved

You need to understand that the market won't be rosy all the time. The market isn't fallible. Heck! Stock prices went down when the New York Stock Exchange was shut down for 136 days during World War I. During this long hiatus, investors counting on capital appreciation from their stocks were disappointed. However, those with dividend stocks kept on receiving their paychecks. So, it is important to place your eggs in the right basket.

You should also keep track of trends and the financial history of the stock you are investing in. In fact, you need to have a firm grip on your financial history in order to build your net worth and manage your money. If you take a look at the Dutch Tulip bubble, the dot.com bubble, and the real estate bubble, you can see that there's isn't much difference between them. Therefore, by arming yourself with these turning points in history, you get to delve into the psychology that influences the selling and buying decisions of individuals. This will help you to avoid financial mistakes that will haunt you and your loved ones. Additionally, mental models are an important tool that you can use to avoid mistakes. In the following chapters, I will show you the strategies you can employ to succeed in investments.

Understand your investments

Do you know that stock funds are different from bond funds, and a stock index fund is not the same as a stock? Most people are generally unaware of the different terms and regulations of investing in the stock market. It is probably not a surprise that Warren Buffet, billionaire and investment guru, made it a rule to never invest in what he does not understand. In other words, it is risky to invest in a niche that's difficult to explain. It's no surprise, then, that Buffet has steered clear of investing heavily in the tech industry. Books are also an excellent way to get information on the stocks you are interested in. Yes, I love the internet and its array of free information; however, nothing beats a good book when you want in-depth knowledge on a particular subject.

Understanding the Stock Market

Are you eager to jump into the world of investments? Perhaps, you've heard of the benefits and million dollars stories in this seemingly magical world of investments. Slow down, as you risk losing your life's investment in an unfamiliar market. For so many new investors, the world of stocks might look like legalized gambling. They think of scenarios like this: if your stock goes up - you win! If it goes down - you lose! How? You don't know since it has become a game of luck. With this type of mentality, the stock market more or less becomes a game of roulette. However, the more you understand the true nature of stocks, the better you will manage your money.

Therefore, in this chapter, you will learn the basic and common terminologies used in the stock market, the reason why companies sell shares, an in-depth analysis of the mechanics of the stock market, and how to recognize a bearish or bullish market. So, let's start with the basic terminologies you will come across while trading in the stock market.

Basic Terminologies Used In the Stock Market

Shares

In the financial market, shares are a unit of capital that depicts the ownership relationship between the shareholder and the company. In such transactions, investors buy or sell shares through a stockbroker who acts as the middleman. The market value of the shares you buy is determined by the performance of the company and other economic factors such as wars, elections, and new economic policies. In addition to this, dividends are the income you earn from shares.

Bonds

Bonds are an interesting alternative to dividend investments. Bonds are defined as fixed income structures that represent a loan made by an individual investor to a borrower. Most times, the borrower is the government or a corporation. Fixed or variable interests rates are attached to these loans, and an end date is fixed for the payment of the principal to the bond owners. Some investors prefer bonds since they are seen as safe, and can be easily traded with other investors or brokers. Companies or other entities issue bonds to investors when they need to raise money for a new project or re-finance an existing debt. They issue bonds that contains the terms and conditions, the time at which the loan (principal) must be paid back, and the interest rates that will be paid. The interest rate is a fixed income that bond owners earn for buying bonds. You should know that the face value or value of bonds differs. In addition to this, you don't have to wait for the bond to expire before you can sell it off.

Equity

In the financial market, the term equity has various definitions. Generally, these definitions revolve around the concept that equity is the difference between the value of assets and liabilities. You can think of equity as the degree of ownership in any asset, once we subtract the cost of the debt associated with it. Here's an example to simplify this term. Imagine you had a car that was worth $15,000, but you owed $5,000 worth of debt against the car. In this case, your equity for the car (asset) was $10,000. Furthermore, equity becomes negative when the cost of liabilities exceeds assets. In terms of shareholder equity or capital, this represents the total number of assets subtracted from liabilities, as divided between shareholders.

Shareholder

You become a shareholder when you own shares of stock in a corporation. Shareholders are the owners of a company since each share of stock they possess entitles them to have a say in the way a corporation operates. However, just because you are a shareholder doesn't mean you can barge in and start firing workers. There are laws in place that protect the company from such actions. Shareholders have the power to elect a board of directors to make major decisions in the company, such as the number of shares to be sold to the public. Besides this, some long-standing corporations pay out dividends to their shareholders.

Initial Public Offering (IPO)

This is a term used to describe the process of a company selling its share of stocks on the stock market for the first time. This is when you hear terms like: "the company is going public." In IPOs, the company's shares are sold to institutional or retail investors, who later sell the shares to other investors via brokers. Investment banks who act as underwriters calculate and establish the value of the company's share, and a detailed overview of the public offering is given to initial investors in the form of a lengthy document known as a prospectus.

Earnings per Share

This is the total profit of the company divided by the number of shares. This is an important factor you must consider before investing in a company. Each part of a company's shares can be likened to pieces of a pie. The larger your share in the corporation, the bigger your pie slices. To know the earnings per share, the investors calculate how much income after tax each share will receive. Therefore, if a company generates more and more profits annually, but only a little profit makes its way to the shareholders on a per-share basis, then it is considered a terrible investment.

Ticker Symbol

Ticker symbols are used to represent corporations listed on the stock market. They are usually a short group of letters. For instance, Johnson & Johnson has a ticker symbol of JNJ and Coca-Cola has a ticker symbol of KO.

Book Value

This is the total asset of a company that's useful to shareholders. It determines what a shareholder will get in case of liquidation. The book value of a company is calculated as the total asset of a company, excluding the liabilities and intangible assets like patents. Investors can use a corporation's book value to gauge if their stocks are over-priced or undervalued.

Corporations

Here's a term that you will come across countless times in this book - corporations are different from businesses. How? Well, any business that sells shares of stocks to investors needs to first become a corporation. A business must undergo a legal process known as incorporation before it becomes a corporation. It's important to understand that a corporation is different from a sole proprietorship or partnership. In fact, it is a virtual person in the eyes of the law. It is registered with the government and has a federal tax number. More so, a corporation can sue, make contracts, and own properties. There are certain laws put in place to ensure uniformity in the way a corporation operates, and how the public and shareholders are protected. For instance, it is compulsory for every corporation to have a board of directors. The shareholders hold yearly meetings to decide who gets to sit on the board. Shareholders also use corporations as shields against liquidity in case the corporation goes bankrupt.

What are Stocks?

Also referred to as equities, stocks are issued by companies in a bid to raise capital in order to expand their business operations or take on new projects. To shareholders, stocks represent a claim of ownership on the company's assets or earnings. Your ownership stake becomes higher as you acquire more stocks. You should know, however, that owning stocks does not give you control over the properties of the corporation, as it is protected under laws of ownership. Now that we've got that out of the way, let's take an in-depth look at the different types of stocks that companies issue to investors.

Types of Stocks

Companies issue two main types of stocks that get listed on the stock market to their investors. It is important to know the type of stock that you are dealing with since each type of stock comes with its own benefits and setbacks. So, let's get right to it!

Common Stocks

When you hear people talking about stocks, it's very likely that they are referring to common stocks. In fact, common stocks make up a large percentage of the total number of stocks traded on the stock market. A common stock confers voting rights on investors, and gives them a right on profits or dividends. With common stocks, investors often get one vote per share to elect a board of directors to oversee operations. What's more, these types of stocks come with higher returns than corporate bonds. However, this high return comes with many risks. If a company goes out of business, you stand to lose your entire life's investment (one of the reasons why you need to diversify). If a company goes out of business (bankrupt) and liquidates, common shareholders will not receive their money until bondholders, preferred stockholders, and creditors have been paid.

Preferred Stocks

Preferred stocks have a similar bill function to bonds, and don't usually come with voting rights. Sometimes, some companies offer voting rights with their preferred stocks. With preferred stocks, investors will get a fixed income in the form of dividends. The dividends are guaranteed, unlike common stocks which have variable dividends that are never guaranteed. In fact, many companies don't pay out dividends to common stockholders. Also, in the case of liquidation, preferred shareholders are paid first, before common shareholders. The company settles creditors and bondholders before getting to preferred stockholders.

What's more? Companies can buy back preferred stocks from shareholders at any time. Therefore, you can consider preferred stocks as a blend of the features of bonds and common stocks. Aside from common stocks and preferred stocks, companies can also create classes of shares in a bid to fit the needs of investors. Companies create classes of stocks when they want to keep power concentrated in a certain group of shareholders.

Why Do Companies Sell Shares?

After examining the core terminologies used in the stock market, it is time to take a look at why companies sell their shares, how stocks are issued, and the role of investors in creating a relationship that will benefit both parties. I'm not going to bore you with a vague or un-interesting description. Instead, we will paint a scenario that you can relate to. So, let's use a pizzeria as our case study.

Will has a pizza business with annual earnings of $350,000. His total after-tax profit is $100,000 per year, which is quite a fair amount. However, Will wants more. He wants to expand his business to a neighboring town, which has more potential and a higher population. So, how does he go about this? First, he calculates the cost of building a new pizzeria. The land and equipment required for the new pizzeria will cost up to $500, 000 upfront. Then, he has to consider the cost of staff, ingredients for the products, and a delivery vehicle to ensure smooth operation. Right now, Will is looking at a sum of $750,000 to cover all his expenses. He is faced with two options; either getting a loan or going public to get funds from investors like you. On one hand, he has to consider the interest that comes with loans, and how he could lose everything if he defaults. In addition to this, banks don't always lend money to companies, especially small businesses. Therefore, he makes the decision to give up a percentage of his ownership control in order to raise cash for his dream. Will invites an underwriter from an investment bank such as JP Morgan or Goldman Sachs to evaluate his total asset, and to set the price for his stocks. As mentioned before, Will's Pizza shop earns $100,000 after-tax profit each year. The company also has a book value of $4 million. Then, the underwriter carries out research and finds out that the average pizza company on the stock market trades for 25 times its company's earnings. Therefore, the underwriter will multiply the company's earnings of $100,000 by 25and add the book value to the result. This means Will's pizza shop is worth $6.5 million.

Will can decide to sell a certain percentage of his stocks to investors in order to meet his financial target. If he sells 40 percent of his company to the public as a stock, this means he gets to keep $3.9 million worth of the business. The underwriters search for investors that will buy the stock, and will ultimately offer Will a check of $2.6 million. With a huge income from sold shares, Will can build not just one but two pizzerias anywhere he wants. On the other hand, investors should expect a minimum profit of at least 10 percent of their investment - it's a win-win for both parties!

This is a scenario that depicts the mutual relationship between shareholders and corporations. Now that we have got that out of the way, let's delve into the basics of the stock market and how to understand its technicalities.

What is the Stock Market?

The stock market is not like your neighborhood grocery store: you can only buy and sell through licensed brokers who make trades on major indexes like Nasdaq and S&P 100. This is where investors meet up to buy and sell stocks or other financial investments like bonds. The stock market is made up of so many exchanges, like the Nasdaq or the New York Exchange. These exchanges are not open all through the day. Most exchanges like the Nasdaq and NYSE are open from 9:30 am to 4pm. EST. Although premarket and trading after closing time now exists, not all brokers do this.

Companies list their stocks on an exchange in a bid to raise money for their business, and investors buy those shares. In addition to this, investors can trade shares among themselves, and the exchange keeps track of the rate of supply and demand of each listed stock. The rate of supply and demand of stocks determines the price. If there's a high demand for a particular stock, its price tends to rise. On the other hand, the price of a stock goes down when there's less demand for it. The stock market computer algorithm handles these varying fluctuations in prices.

How Does The Stock Market Work?

A Stock market analysis definitely looks like gibberish to

beginners and average investors. However, you should know that the way this market works is actually quite simple. Just imagine a typical auction house or an online auction website. This market works in the same way - it allows buyers and sellers to negotiate prices and carry out successful trades. The first stock market took place in a physical marketplace, however, these days, trades happen electronically via the internet and online stockbrokers. From the comfort of your homes, you can easily bid and negotiate for the prices of stocks with online stockbrokers.

Furthermore, you might come across news headlines that say the stock market has crashed or gone up. Once again, don't fret or get all excited when you come across such news. Most often than not, this means a stock market index has gone up or down. In other words, the stocks in a market index have gone down. Before we proceed, let's explore the meaning of market indexes.

Stock Market Indexes

As mentioned earlier, when people refer to the rise and fall of the stock market, they are generally referring to one of the major stock market's market indexes. Market indexes track the performance of a group of stocks in a particular sector like manufacturing or technology. The value of the stocks featured in an index is representative of all the stocks in that sector. It is very important to take note of what stocks each market index represents. As mentioned in the first chapter, you should invest in a niche you are comfortable with. In addition to this, giant market indexes like the Dow Jones Industrial Average, the Nasdaq composite, and the Standard & Poor's 500, are often used as proxies for the performance of the stock market as a whole. You can choose to invest in an entire index through the exchange-traded funds and index funds, as it can track a specific sector or index of the stock market.

Bullish and Bearish Markets

Talking about the bullish outlook of the stock market is guaranteed to get beginners looking astonished. Yes, it sounds ridiculous at first, but with time, you get to appreciate the ingenuity of these descriptions. Let's start with the bearish market. A bear is ananimal you would never want to meet on a hike; it strikes fear into your heart, and that's the effect you will get from a bearish market. A bear market depicts when stock prices are falling across several of the indexes mentioned earlier. The threshold for a bearish market varies within a 20 percent loss or more.

Most young investors unfamiliar with a bear market as we've been in a bull market since the first quarter of 2019. In fact, this makes it the second-longest bull market in history. Just as you have probably guessed by now, a bull market indicates that stock prices are rising. You should know that the market is continually changing from bull to bear and vice versa. From the Great Recession to the global market crash, these changing market prices indicate the start of larger economic patterns. For instance, a bull market shows that investors are investing heavily and that the economy is doing extremely well. On the other hand, a bear market shows investors are scared and pulling back, with the economy on the brink of collapsing. If this made you paranoid about the next bear market, don't fret. Business analysts have shown that the average bull market generally outlasts the average bear market by a large margin. This is why you can grow your money in stocks over an extended period of time.

Stock Market Corrections and Crash

A stock market crash is every investor's nightmare. It is usually extremely difficult to watch stocks that you've spent so many years accumulating diminish before your very eyes. Yes, this is how volatile the stock market is. Stock market crashes usually include a very sudden and sharp drop in stock prices, and it might herald the beginning of a bear market. On the other hand, stock market corrections occur when the market drops by 10 percent - this is just the market's way of balancing itself. The current bull market has gone through 5 market corrections.

Analyzing the Stock Market

You are not psychic. It is nearly impossible to accurately predict the outcome of your stock to the last detail. However, you can become near perfect at reading the stock market by learning how to properly analyze the components of this market. There are two basic types of analyses: technical analysis and fundamental analysis.

Fundamental Market Analysis

Fundamental analysis involves getting data about a company's stocks or a particular sector in the stock market, via financial records, company assets, economic reports, and market share. Analysts and investors can conduct fundamental analysis via the metrics on a corporation's financial statement. These metrics include but are not limited to cash flow statements, balance sheet statements, footnotes, and income statements. Most times, you can get a company's financial statement through a 10-k report in the database. In addition to this, the SEC's EDGAR is a good place to get the financial statement of the company you are interested in. With the financial statement, you can deduce the revenues, expenses, and profits a company has made.

What's more? By looking at the financial statement, you will have a measure of a company's growth trajectory, leverage, liquidity, and solvency. Analysts utilize different ratios to make an accurate prediction about stocks. For example, the quick ratio and current ratio are useful in determining if a company will be able to pay its short-term liabilities with the current asset. If the current ratio is less than 1, the company is in poor financial health and may not be able to recover from its short-term debt. Here's another example: a stock analyst can use the debt ratio to measure the current level of debt taken on by the company. If the debt ratio is above 1, it means the company has more debt than assets and it's only a matter of time before it goes under.

Technical Market Analysis

This is the second part of stock market analysis and it revolves around studying past market actions to predict the stock price direction. Technical analysts put more focus on the price and volume of shares. Additionally, they analyze the market as a whole and study the supply and demand factors that dictate market movement. In technical analyses, charts are of inestimable value. Charts are a vital tool as they show the graphical representation of a stock's trend within a set time frame. What's more? Technical investors are able to identify and mark certain areas as resistance or support levels on a chart. The resistance level is a previous high stock price before the current price. On the other hand, support levels are represented by a previous low before the current stock price. Therefore, a break below the support levels marks the beginning of a bearish trend. Alternatively, a break above the resistance level marks the beginning of a bullish market trend. A technical analysis is only effective when the rise and fall of stock prices are influenced by supply and demand forces. However, a technical analysis is mostly rendered ineffective in the face of outside forces that affect stock prices such as stock splits, dividend announcements, scandals, changes in management, mergers, and so on. Investors can make use of both types of analyses to get an accurate prediction of their stock values.

Why You Need To Diversify

According to research by Ned Davis, a bear market occurs every 3.5 years and has an average lifespan of 15 months. One thing is clear, though: you can't avoid bear markets. You can, however, avoid the risks that come with investing in a single investment portfolio. Let's look at a common mistake that new investors typically make. Research points to the fact that individual stocks dwindle to a loss of 100 percent. By throwing in your lot with one company, you are exposing yourself to many setbacks. For example, you can lose your money if a corporation is embroiled in a scandal, poor leadership, and regulatory issues. So, how can you balance out your losses? By investing in the aforementioned index fund or ETF fund, as these indexes hold many different stocks, as by doing this, you've automatically diversified your investment. Here's a nugget to cherish: put 90 percent of your investment funds in an index fund, and put the remaining 10 percent in an individual stock that you trust.

When to Sell Your Stocks

One thing is sure - you are not going to hold your stocks forever. All our investment advice and energies are directed towards buying. Yes, it is the buying of stocks that kick-start the whole investment when chasing your dream concept. However, just as every beginning has an end, you will eventually sell every stock you buy. It is the natural order. Even so, selling off stock is not an easy decision. Heck! It's even harder to determine the right time to sell. This is the point where greed and human emotions start to battle with pragmatism. Many investors try to make sensible selling decisions solely based on price movements. However, this is not a sure strategy, as it is still sensible to hold onto a stock that has fallen in value. Conversely, selling a stock when it has reached your target is seen as prudent. So, how can you navigate around this dilemma? Before touching on other parts in this section, let's first tackle the reason why selling is so hard.

Why Selling Is So Hard

Do you know why it's so hard to let go of your stocks even when you have a fixed strategy to follow? The answer lies in human greed. When making decisions, it's an innate human tendency to be greedy. Here's an example: an investor purchases shares at $30, and tells herself that when the stocks hit $40, she will sell. Here comes an all-too-familiar trend - when the stocks finally hit $40, the investor will hold out and see if her stock prices will rise beyond $40. You can see that human nature is already creeping in. Surely, the stocks hit $45, and greed takes over logical thinking. She decides to wait to see if it rises beyond $45. Suddenly, the stock prices plummet down to $36. At this point, she tells herself that once the stocks rise again to $40, she will sell. Unfortunately, this never happens. This stock continues to plummet down to $25. Finally, she succumbs to her frustrations and sells at $25.

From the above example, you can see how greed and irrationality took over her sound investment plan. In this scenario, sound investment plans were replaced with gambling tendencies. Although the investment was a loss at $5 per share, her true loss stands at $20 per share. This is because she had the opportunity to sell at $45 but she held out, hoping for even higher prices. Knowing when to sell is truly a paramount factor. Sometimes, a good selling decision that brings some profits to your table might look like a poor selling decision. However, in this scenario, it's advised to say prudent. To remove human emotions from your decisions, you can consider adding a limit order which automatically locks in your selling decision. The limit order will sell once it reaches your target price.

Wait! Ask Yourself These Questions before Selling Your Shares

You have held out long enough, and you feel it's time to take the big leap. Perhaps, you have seen the haphazard rise and fall of stock prices, and you don't want to be at the short end of the stick. Hold on! Ask yourself these questions before you sell.

Is the company suffering from any setback?

Today, we have access to more information than ever. As you have nonstop access to the internet, it can be extremely difficult not to constantly check market data. However, beware that doing this can make you succumb to emotional triggers, and this might ultimately lead to poor selling decisions. The best thing you can do in this situation is to get some perspective. Compare the company's total revenues to its benchmark and to others in the same sector. This can help you to discern if the slow performance is an indication of falling stock prices, or just a random market movement.

Is your portfolio out of balance?

As an ideal investor, you have diversified your investment across various sectors. Over time, some stocks begin to perform better than others in that portfolio, making your investments shift towards the out-performers. Therefore, it is necessary to bring your investments back in line to conform to your fixed asset plan. In this situation, you are faced with two options to even the scales: you either buy more of the stocks that have fallen behind or sell the outperforming stocks.

Will you get a tax break?

Yes, your investments have reached your target price and you can wait to sell. Before you do, remember that selling a stock that has increased in a tax-prone brokerage account can trigger a tax bill. The rate of the tax depends on whether you have held the investment for more than a year. If you have, you are eligible for a reduced long-term capital tax rate. If not, you will attract higher short-term tax rates.

Is there a better investment for your money?

According to billionaire investor and guru, Warren Buffet, the best holding time is forever. However, that's pretty unrealistic for an investor with a finite income. Sometimes, we sell off investments in order to meet up with certain needs such as retirement, college funds, vacations, and anything else that requires capital. Admittedly, it's a wise choice to selloff stocks to meet up with current cash needs and to avoid the volatility of the market. However, I advise not to use your long-term funds for your immediate needs.

How will you make your exit?

Once again, you are not psychic. It is nearly impossible to time a perfect sale - you don't know when a stock is at its lowest point or when it's at its highest point. Running to sell off your stocks can save you from losing more, and it also denies you the opportunity to gain additional income if the stock rises. Those are the uncertainties that you have to deal with as an investor. However, there's a trick to selling your shares. You can sell shares at different time periods. If you sell them all at once, you might lose out on additional opportunities. If the stock has a good potential, then you should sell part of it and hold on to the rest.

Introduction to Dividend Investment

What is Dividend Investment?

Generally speaking, dividends are referred to as the distribution of after-tax earnings of a company to shareholders in relation to the number of shares they hold. Mind you, there are 3 parts to this definition, and each one is equally important. Firstly, dividends are paid from profit and not from any other source of equity, for instance, paid-in surplus. Secondly, dividends must be in the form of real assets, and this part is quite tricky. It is a common habit for companies to pay out dividends in the form of cash, checks, or more stocks, since these are convenient. However, it would be quite difficult and nonsensical for an airline company like Boeing to offer the right wing of a 747 to a major shareholder as dividends. Nevertheless, during high levels of inflation, we have seen corporations pay dividends in the form of products that they sell. Finally, the third part of this definition states that every shareholder has a share in dividends irrespective of the number of shares that they hold in the company.

So, How Did It All Start?

You might wonder: how did companies start paying dividends and who started the whole concept? Well, dividend-paying stocks have been around for hundreds of years, and it has provided an infallible source of passive income to investors for many generations. Here's the outline of the history of dividend-paying stocks.

1250

A French bank called Société des Moulins du Bazacle was the first company to pay out dividends.

1602

Nearly 400 years later, the Dutch East India Company became the second corporation in history to pay out dividends. Over the course of its 200-year existence, this company paid out 18 percent of its capital.

1682

Dividend investment finally officially came to North America. The Hudson Bay Company is arguably the first to pay dividends; the first dividends were paid about 14 years after the inception of the company in 1670and were worth half of the stock value.

1910

In the early 20th century, many investors were only interested in stocks paying dividends. During this period, stocks were expected to have higher dividend yields than bonds in order to compensate investors for the risks that come with most equities.

2003

After 28 years of growth, tech giant Microsoft declares its first dividend payment.

Today, about 420 companies out of the 500 company stocks on the S&P 500 pay a dividend. This includes giant corporations like Chevron, McDonalds, and Wal-Mart.

Terms to Know In Dividend Investment

Before we proceed into the countless benefits of dividend investments as a passive income, here are a few terms you first need to get familiar with. These terms will not help you to breach the world of dividends but will enable you to make better financial decisions during investments. You are bound to come across many of these terms in the next chapter.

Cash Dividends

Cash dividends are cash payments made to shareholders as part of the company's accumulated earnings or current profit. This is a way for the company to return profits to investors for the shares they hold. Companies pay out dividends monthly, quarterly or yearly. Besides normal dividend payouts, shareholders can also receive special cash dividends after legal settlements or a one-time cash distribution.

Declaration Date

This is the date on which the board of directors in a corporation announces the next dividend payment. Also referred to as the announcement date, the board of directors announces the ex-dividend date, the dividend size, and the payment date.

Dividend Cover Ratio

The Dividend Cover Ratio is the ratio between a company's net dividend to shareholders and its earnings. This is an analytical tool used by investors to gauge if a company's earnings can sufficiently cover its dividends to investors. You can calculate this by dividing the earnings per share by the dividends per share.

Dividend Reinvestment Plan (DRIP)

This is a plan offered to investors by dividend-paying corporations to re-invest their cash dividends. The DRIP is an amazing strategy that you will come across in the course of this book. By re-investing your cash dividends into more shares, you will earn higher dividend payouts. Furthermore, most Dividend Reinvestment Plans allow investors to buy additional shares at a discount and without commission, however, most DRIPdon't allow a reinvestment that's less than $10. If your company doesn't offer a DRIP, you can set one up with a major brokerage firm.

Dividend Yield

Dividend yield is a term you definitely need to add to your repertoire. It is a financial ratio that, in relation to its share value, depicts the amount a company pays out in dividend each year. You can measure the dividend yield by dividing the yearly dividend per share by the share price. This term represents the total amount of return from an investment, and it's the perfect tool to measure potential investments.

Here's how to calculate a dividend yield. Let's assume Company ABC is trading at $40 per share and the company offers a yearly dividend of $1.5 per share. Therefore, the dividend yield would be at 3.75%. You may have noticed that the share price and dividend yield move in the opposite direction. If we selected a higher share price of $60, for example, the dividend yield would decrease (1.48 dividend ÷ $60 per share equals to 2.45% yield). Therefore, you can earn more dividend income if the share price is lower.

Record Date

Companies determine their shareholders on the record date.

Ex-dividend Date

The ex-dividend date is one of the four main important dates to dividend investors. This is the fixed duration on or after which a security is traded without a formerly announced distribution or dividend. Additionally, it is also the date on which the seller of a stock will be entitled to a recently declared dividend.

Payment Date

This is the date on which a stock dividend is scheduled to be paid to shareholders. You should know that only those who bought their shares before the ex-dividend date can receive dividends on the payment date.

One-time Dividends

Also referred to as special dividends, these payments are larger than the conventional dividends paid out to shareholders.

Rules of Dividend Investments

Dividend investments, just like any other niche, comes with its own set of rules. Think of these rules as short-cuts to avoid making common mistakes. These rules are backed by academic research and principles from some of the world's greatest investors. Mind you, don't think of these rules as infallible since there will be always be an exception. Nevertheless, it's good to integrate these rules into your everyday investment decisions.

Always Go For Quality!

Long-term orientation is one of the best advantages an investor could ever have. It is a rule to invest in businesses that have stability, profit, and a proven track record showing growth. Why should you go for a mediocre business when you can invest in a high-quality business? As a financial rule, you should rank stocks by both their dividend and corporate history length, and the longer they are, the better.

The Bargain Principle

It is a rule to invest in businesses that pay you the most dividends for the cash you invest. Remember, the higher the dividend yield, the better. In addition to this, avoid investing in overpriced securities. You should only deal with stocks trading below a decade historical average valuation multiple, which is the average value of stocks calculated over a ten-year period.

Always Play Safe

Avoid businesses that pay out all their income as dividends, as this means that the business has no margin of safety, and dividends can be reduced at any time.

Reinvest Your Dividends

This is definitely one rule you must never break. The power of reinvesting your dividends cannot be undermined. In fact, putting your dividends back to work can do wonders for your portfolio. What's more? You can make use of reinvestment programs, which often enable you to reinvest your payouts automatically without paying a commission fee.

Understand Your Tax Laws

Warren Buffet once said that he is taxed less than his secretary. So, how does he do it? Well, most of his income comes from dividends, which are indeed often taxed, though lower than standard income. So, get familiar with the tax structure for dividends and take note of any changes resulting from new company or government policies.

Don't Make Dividends Your Only Priority

Dividends are an indispensable part of investing. However, dividends are not the all-mighty metric to abide by. Investors need to pay attention to different fundamentals that are often at play in investments. Fundamentals like profits, price actions, and earning growths are just a few of the features you need to pay attention to. Remember to look beyond high-dividend yields and ensure you understand the company's growth pattern and future prospects.

Watch Out For Value Traps

Many investors jump at seemingly lucrative stocks without realizing that they are value traps. A value trap is a phenomenon where a dividend yield is increasing and stock prices are reducing. When faced with this phenomenon, most investors think they've hit the jackpot. However, they fail to realize that the stock prices were reducing for a legitimate reason. So, how can you detect this trap before it is too late? Here's the first sign to watch out for. When you see a company that pays out far more than its peers in the sector or market index, this indicates a value trap. In addition to this, falling cash flows with stable yields also indicate a value trap.

Always Look Out For Special Dividends

One of the perks of dividend investments is the ability of corporations to initiate a one-time dividend payout. When looking for stocks to purchase, these one-time dividend payouts often mislead investors. During one-time dividend payments, a company's stock might seem rosier than normal. A good example is Microsoft (MSFT), who issued a one-time dividend payment in 2004 which was a sharp contrast to the normal dividend payouts. Microsoft's normal dividend payouts varied from $0.3 to $0.5, while the one-time dividend payout was a whopping $3 per share. Many resources calculate the one-time dividend payment as an annual yield. If we were to include the special dividend payout, Microsoft's annual yield for 2004 would have been 13.78%, instead of the 0.38% payout from normal dividends. As you can see, the figure was enough to confuse investors who hadn't checked and analyzed the yield statistics.

Use the Survival of the Fittest Principle

Sell your stocks when your dividend payouts are reduced or cut short - it's that simple. Research carried out between 1972 and 2017 showed that stocks that cut or reduced their dividend payouts had a 0% percent recovery. If your dividends are reduced or stopped, this obviously goes against the principles of generating passive income. In fact, it is the opposite of what we are aiming for. Any business that cuts its dividends has lost its competitive advantage. Therefore, you want to reinvest the proceeds of your sale into a more profitable stock.

Using Dividends as a Passive Income

According to research by Ned Davis, a bear market occurs every 3.5 years, and has occurred 32 times in 118 years. What's more? According to Azzad Asset management, an average bear market lasts for 15 months with stock prices declining by more than 30 percent. The most recent bear market, for example, lasted for 17 months. What's the point of looking at these statistics? For some investors, a bear market and market crashes are unavoidable. However, some investors are immune to the fluctuations in the stock market. Yes, you heard that right. Those who invest in dividends are not affected by the rise and fall of share prices. In fact, they continue to receive their monthly or annual dividends even when the stock market falls, and this feature is why dividend investment is the best passive income for you. Contrary to general opinions, dividends and other paying stocks are not restricted to those close to the age of retirement. Instead, it's the ideal passive income investment for everyone, irrespective of age or stage in life. Passive investments are ideal for those who want to retain their capital but still earn regular income. Yes, buying investment stocks allows you to earn dividends while your stock value appreciates. As you continue reading, you will understand the basics of dividend investments and how you can effectively navigate the market via solid strategies.

Misconceptions of Dividend Investment

In the introduction, I placed emphasis on the word "dream." The dream of a better life - endless vacations, a new house, a new car, and so on. Yes, these dreams are the reason why we aim to boost our earnings through passive income. It is probably even the reason why you are reading this book. However, you should understand that there is a multitude of misconceptions surrounding dividends which might lead to unrealistic expectations. So, let's take a look at the common misconceptions around this niche.

High Yields Are a Priority

Why don't we start with the biggest misconception of dividends investment—that high yields are always a good thing. This is a trap that most new investors fall for - they simply choose a list of high paying stocks and just wait and hope for the best. High paying stocks are not always what they paint out to be. Let's take a look at a list of monthly paying stocks. When you peruse this list of companies with the highest dividend yields, the top names on this list are not always the top performers on a return basis. What does this mean? In the third quarter of 2018, Corus Entertainment is at the top of the list of companies with high dividend yields, with 26.9 percent. However, when you look a little deeper, you see that this company has a three-year annualized accumulated return of - 18.54 percent, and a ten-year annualized accumulative return of - 1.81 percent. Remember, a dividend is a fraction of a company's profit paid out to investors, and any money paid out as dividends cannot be re-invested. Therefore, if a company pays out a large percentage of its profits as dividends, this surely means that it has little space for growth. You should understand that the market has no place for stagnant companies. What's more? You can't avoid investing in such companies by studying its dividend payout ratio, as the ratio measures the percentage of profits paid out to shareholders. Mind you, some sectors in the stock market have high payouts since this is part of their corporate structure. Master limited partnerships and real estate trusts are prime examples of these sectors. These companies have high dividend yields and payout ratios as it's integrated into their structure.

Dividend Stocks are Boring

Here's another misconception that we have to discard. Dividend stocks are far from boring if you take away the importance of yields. When we talk about high yield dividends, most people tend to think of utility companies. These companies generally lack the excitement of fluctuating stock prices during dividend announcements. The announcement of new dividends generates much excitement, and this can jolt the stock price of a share. Sure, it's difficult to predict a company's new dividends and whether the stock prices will go up. However, you can read the trend by looking at the following indicators:

Financial Flexibility

A corporation has room to increase its dividend if its stock has a low dividend payout ratio, but is generating high levels of cash flow. On the other hand, it is a bad sign if a company is taking out loans to maintain its dividend payments.

Organic growth

Here's a nugget you should always watch out for. It isn't enough to simply watch out for earning growth. It is important to observe revenues and cash flows, too. If a company is showing signs of organic growth (increased sales, margin, and traffic), it is only a matter of time before the dividend payout increases. There is, however, a clause to this indicator. If a company's growth stems from an international expansion or investment in high-risk sectors, then an increase in dividend payout is uncertain.

Dividends are Safe

Since the start of this book, I have made sure to hammer-in one point: dividend investment is not a get-rich-quick scheme. Here's another important point: dividends are not always safe. I know this might generate some uncertainties, but let me elaborate. Dividend stocks are well known for being reliable and safe investments. In fact, dividend experts have collated a list of "safe" companies that have increased their dividend payouts over the last quarter of a century. Taking a look into the S&P 100 market index, which features a list of the most established and stable companies in the US, you will find a plethora of safe and progressing dividend-paying companies.

However, just because a company pays out dividends, this doesn't necessarily make it a safe bet. We have had safe, solid companies like General Motors, Bank of America, and Pfizer that were considered safe bets by investors, cut or suspend their dividend payouts. Over time, company managements have always used dividends to soothe or placate investors even when stocks are not moving - I call these strategies "dividend traps." In order to avoid dividend traps, you should always consider that a company is utilizing dividends in its corporate strategy. It is a bad idea to give dividends as consolation prizes to investors when stock prices are not moving. In 2008, there was mass hysteria when the stock market plunged down; this was also the period when dividend payouts were increased artificially, in a bid to make up for the decline in stock prices. Although these dividends looked attractive at first, they were completely cut off due to the financial crisis. Furthermore, the sudden cut-off of dividend caused a crash in the stock market.

Dividends Guarantee Downside Protection and Upside Potentials

Let's look at these common misconceptions on dividends. Some analysts, while trying to boost the benefits of dividends, said that dividends help to offset depreciation in market price that occurs during the financial crisis. I'd tell you this, "Dividends just offer a little shock absorption against crashing stock prices. Here's an example: During the late 2008 to early 2009 market crash, the S&P 500 was down -41.82%. Also, the SPDR S&P 500 dividend fund was down by - 35.87%. This is a downside protection of just 6.1% ,which is quite small. Furthermore, some popular dividend-centric funds performed even worse than the S&P 500 during that period.

By looking beyond the dividend yield, You can become a top investor. When making an investment, you can combine factors such as the total returns with the dividend yields. In addition to this, try not to narrow your searches just to safe dividend-paying companies that have been on the market for 25 years. Instead, you can look towards emerging companies that show the potential to bring in great returns.

Why Is Dividend Investment So Powerful?

The truth is; dividend investment doesn't have the headline-grabbing power that other parts of investment do. It's not exactly a fun topic to bring up at a dinner party. Why? Well, it's understandable that the topic of dividend investment has failed to generate excitement, as in the days of fast-rising tech stocks like Amazon, Facebook, and Netflix, people are not so keen to see the beauty of dividend-bearing stocks - it just doesn't hold that appeal. However, there's a secret to investing in dividends, and that's the power of compound interest. We will talk about this concept in more detail in another sub-section. At a glance, compound interest is the interest you get on capital, and on the accumulated interest on previous interests. Just think of it as an unending cycle of earning interest upon interest, and this can quickly "snowball" into a huge sum in the future. For instance, you invested $10,000 dollars in Coca-Cola in 1962, and you re-invested the dividends you got from your capital into the company. By 2012, which is half a century later, your investment would have yielded $2 million. Now, that's a hefty sum, if you ask me.

Also, dividends are so great because they don't just generate cash flow for you, but also protect you from inflation and a volatile market. Since 1912, dividends have increased by 4.2% and inflation increased 3.3%. As you can see, your investments are well protected. In addition to this, dividend yields increase as the stock market falls.

Why Do Companies Pay Dividends?

As we have seen, dividends are powerful tools for generating passive income. In the previous section, I gave an example of someone investing a mere $10,000 in Coca-Cola in 1962, and the portfolio increased to $2 million in 50 years. Well, this is just the tip of the proverbial iceberg that we call "dividend investments." Do you know that dividend-paying companies also provide different tax benefits for investors? There's no doubt that this is a great option for you. While pondering on this, have you ever given a thought to why companies pay dividends? This is a very important point, as most people miss out on the purpose of dividends, and that's why some companies pay and others don't. Before we begin to describe the various policies that companies use to determine what to pay their investors, let's take a look at the argument against dividends by financial companies and analysts.

Arguments against Dividends

Let's face it: dividend investment is not the coolest pupil in the school of investments. Major tech corporations like Amazon and Facebook have refused to pay dividends despite netting massive returns each year. Even Berkshire Hathaway, the Holding company for billionaire guru and investor Warren Buffet, does not have a dividend paying company in its holdings. Many top-shot investors have come out and denounced the importance of dividends when it comes to making money on the stock market.

According to Sameer Sama, a technical and global equity strategist at the Wells Fargo Investment Institute in St. Louis, "once a company starts paying a dividend, investors get used to it and it can then be hard to eliminate or reduce them. Therefore, many companies prefer to choose special dividends, which can be much more discretionary."

Financial analysts like Sameer Sana, also argue that that

little to no dividend payment is favorable for an investor. In their defense, they point out that the taxation of dividends is more than that of capital gain. They also believe that it is better for a company to re-invest their funds instead of paying out dividendsbecause if corporations re-invest their funds, their market value will increase and this will also boost their stock value. The proponents of this school of thought believe that a company's alternatives to paying out part of their profits as dividends are the following: re-investing in financial assets, acquiring new assets, and re-purchasing the company's own shares.

Arguments for Dividends

Despite this overwhelming lackluster attitude towards the concept of dividends, let's take a look at companies that do pay dividends. This will help us to discard the argument that companies can't increase their stock value if they pay out dividends. To discredit this, let's look at 2 major corporations, 3M.Co and Johnson and Johnson.3M.Co (MMM) has enjoyed over 60 years of paying a dividend to investors. Today, its dividend per share sits at $4.70, and this rate is double what the company paid in 2012. Johnson and Johnson (JnJ) is another example of a company that continues to pay dividends to investors since the days of President Kennedy. Thanks to ground-breaking products, their stocks have risen by 45 percent in the last 5 years. What's more? Their shares now sell for $125.

So, why do these companies keep dishing out dividends despite the arguments against them? They do so as it provides certainty about their financial well-being; there's definitely no investor that would doubt the financial capabilities of a company that pays dividends. It's probably the reason why only strong and long-standing corporations pay out dividends. To many investors, it's an indication of a company with a strong market value. In addition to this, corporations in this category are attractive to investors looking for current income. Also, company stocks are bound to rise when there's an increase in the dividend payouts to investors. This brings us to our next section: how companies pay out dividends.

How Companies Pay Out Dividends

You should know that there are different types of dividends, and each comes with a myriad of benefits and setbacks. Therefore, as an investor, it is important to take note of the types of dividends that a company is dishing out, as this will save you money and unnecessary stress. When a corporation decides to either pay a high or low dividend, it would do so with one of five main approaches:

- Residual Dividends
- Stability Dividends
- Hybrid (a blend of residual and stability dividends)
- Stock Dividends
- Property Dividends

Residual Dividends

The residual dividend policy is quite an interesting concept, and it's easy to understand. Companies using the residual dividend policy prefer to rely on their internal generated equity to finance new projects. For instance, the company might decide to upgrade its machinery in order to boost the production rate and increase revenues. After financing the project, the company will attempt to balance their debt to equity ratio before distributing any dividends. Mind you, the company will not distribute any dividend if there is no leftover revenue.

Let's look at an example to better understand this concept.

Imagine that Company ABC has recently earned $10,000, and it has a strict policy to always keep a debt to equity ratio of 0.5. This means that for every debt, there will be twice the amount of equity. Now, let's say this company needs to buy or upgrade an asset that requires a capital of $9,000. To maintain its debt to equity ratio of 0.5, the company will have to pay for one-third of the cost of this asset by using debt ($3,000), and the remaining two-thirds of the cost of the asset by using equity ($6,000). In simpler terms, the company will borrow $3,000 and use $6,000 of its equity to buy the asset in order to maintain the debt/equity ratio of 0.5. This will leave the company with $4,000, and this will serve as the residual dividend paid out to shareholders. On the other hand, investors might not receive any residual dividend when the cost of financing a new project is higher than their equity. In this case, the board of directors will come up with detailed explanations as to why they were unable to give out dividends.

Stability Dividends

The concept of stability dividends is quite a sharp contrast to residual dividends. Residual dividends are unstable and fluctuate in the face of market conditions and company policies, whereas a stability dividends policy is set at stable prices, and its aim is to reduce uncertainties for investors. Therefore, investors don't have to worry whether they will get the next dividend check or not, as is common with residual dividends. In stability dividends policies, the company might decide to select a cyclical policy that sets the dividends at a fixed percentage of the yearly earnings. On the other hand, it could choose a stable policy where quarterly dividends are fixed at a percentage of the yearly earnings.

Let's look at an example. Our imaginary company, XYZ, has yearly earnings of $10,000 from quarterly earnings of $4,000, $2,000, $1,000, and $3,000. Then, Company XYZ decides to pay a stable dividend policy of 10% out of its yearly earnings. This means it will pay $250 to shareholders every quarter, leading to a total sum of $1,000 per year. Alternatively, if the company decides on a cyclic dividend policy, the dividend payment will fluctuate to accommodate the change in the quarterly earnings. Therefore, the earnings for each quarter are $400, $200, $100, and $300. In either instance, the company is trying to share its revenue with the shareholders, in a bid to foster trust and more cooperation. In addition to this, it grants them a strong financial stance in the stock market.

Hybrid Dividend

The hybrid dividend policy merges both the residual and stability dividend policies together. Many corporations use this approach when paying out dividends. Through this approach, they tend to view the debt to equity ratio as long-term rather than short term. The reason for this is that companies often have to battle uncertain economic policies that may affect their operations. Therefore, they will have a fixed set of dividends which will represent a small fraction of their yearly income, which is easily maintained. In addition to this, they will offer another set of dividends that will act as a residual dividend policy which will be paid only when income exceeds the required levels.

Stock Dividends

The first two dividends are referred to as cash dividends since investors receive residual or stability dividend policies in real assets. Stock dividends, though, are completely different.

For instance, let's say a company declares 20% stock dividends. An investor with 100 shares would receive an additional 20, bringing it to a total of 120 shares. At this point, new investors will jump for joy since they think their stakes have increased. However, they haven't really increased since the total market value hasn't changed. Here's why: if the investor owned 1% of the company before the stock dividends, he/she will still hold the same amount after the stock dividend. The only change in this situation is the change in the price of his shares. Since he owns 20% more shares, his share price will reduce by 20 percent. Stock dividend policy is just like a mini stock split - it does not add any value to the investor. You should know that this method of dividend payout is becoming obsolete, with a decline in the number of companies using it. Companies usually undertake this method to enable to direct its earnings towards developing the firm via internal growth. In addition, they also use this method to reduce the distribution of cash to investors. This would allow the company to use its new debt and retained cash to fund a new acquisition. Coca-Cola did just that in 1988 - it spun off its subsidiary, Columbia Pictures to its shareholders. This means that for each share of Coca-Cola that an investor owned, he would receive 0.092 share of the subsidiary. Fractional shares occur due to a merger, acquisition, stock split, or spin-off. Furthermore, they are difficult to sell off unless you do so via a major brokerage firm, which would pair each partial sale with another.

Property Dividends

The concept of property dividends is another non-monetary dividend policy. In this case, the payouts have no monetary value. For example, corporation ABC might decide to have 500 shareholders. The corporation has 500 signed Warhol prints, which have been in its vault for years. The total market value of the prints is $500,000. Therefore, the company may decide to give out a print to each of its major shareholders. So, you know that the print is, therefore, worth $500. An investor might decide to sell off the print to get the monetary value of the print, or he may wish to hold on to it for long-term capital gains.

Snowball Effect; Harnessing the Power of Reinvestment

Warren Buffet, "My wealth has come from living in America, some lucky genes, and compound interest"

Do you know about the snowball on the hill metaphor? As it rolls down the hill, the snowball increases in size and gains momentum. The bigger it gets, the more snow it it gathers, getting increasingly bigger with every roll. This description perfectly describes the income compound investment over many years.

Yes, it all boils down to compound interest. At first, the earnings increase by an inch, before slowly gaining momentum and increasing exponentially. Compound interest is definitely not suited to those who are impatient or ruled by their emotions - it is for those who are willing to stay strong during the stormy conditions of the stock market. Just like a snowball rolling down a hill, you have to watch your income run its course in order to reach your financial goal. As I mentioned earlier, dividend investment will not make you rich overnight, you have to let it run its course. Take a look at the life of the investment guru, Warren Buffet. He is definitely not the smartest investor or analyst out there. What's more? He has made many mistakes, some that have seen him lose huge chunks of money. But do you know the one principle he never changed? The principle of snowball effect or compound interest!

In this chapter, you will learn how to harness this power for yourself. However, this power will be ineffective if you don't know the right companies to invest in. Therefore, I will use the names of real-life companies that can help you to boost your passive income. In addition to this, I'll show you what you need to watch out for when choosing companies to invest in.

How to Choose Companies to Invest In

Selecting a good company to invest in is arguably one of the most life-changing decisions you will ever make. There are just countless companies with attractive stock packages. Your broker might be pushing towards one direction while books you may have read are pushing you towards another. Yes, it can get confusing. Therefore, I have painstakingly collated these pointers to help you make better and wiser decisions when selecting companies to invest in.

Choose Companies that Dominate Their Industries

Have you ever noticed that the names of the same companies keep cropping up in different portfolios? Trust me; this is not some conspiracy theory. The companies keep showing up in different subject matter from individual portfolios designed by analysts to mutual funds to index funds. It is not uncommon to see names like Facebook, Apple, Amazon, Coca-Cola, and McDonald's over and over again.

You should know that this is not some dumb luck or coincidence; it's simply because these companies dominate their respective niches. Not only do they have a long track record of industry domination, but they also have an eerie success with every product or service they offer. This is not an accident. These companies have the expertise, capital, and energy to churn out innovative products and services. There's no guarantee that they will continue to do so. However, the fact that they've been doing it consistently in the past is a great indication of continued success.

Only Invest In Businesses You Understand

There is a broad spectrum of companies that you can buy stocks in. At one end of the spectrum are well-known companies that sell goods and services -these are the companies you should invest in. In the financial market, there's a close relationship between the performance of a company's stock, and the success of its products and services. When a product is common, it is used and therefore understood by the public, and if you use the company's products, you already have a good understanding of how the company works.

At the middle of the broad spectrum are the companies in industries you already have a fair understanding of. You may have worked in this industry in the past, or you have a particular interest in it. At the end of this spectrum are the companies that you don't understand at all. I'll advise you to stay away from those. Most of these companies sell ideas alone, and they are not profitable until they make a product that has a breakthrough. Mind you, you can still support these new innovative businesses, but I will advise you not to place the bulk of your investments in them. Invest wisely.

Don't Limit Your Investments to Two or Three Sectors

Here's a disclaimer on the first two points in this section.

Yes, I understand that you want to invest in companies that you understand. However, you should not concentrate your investments on a small number of companies that you are familiar with. For instance, you may be tempted to overload your stocks in the tech industry if you are familiar with the mechanics of this sector. However, you should know that every industry is subject to the rise and fall of the stock market. So, what can you do? If you have 10 different stocks, for example, invest in six to seven different industries. The worst thing you can do is to accumulate around half of your stocks in a single industry. Yes, it might serve you well when the industry is flourishing, but on the other hand, the backlash might wreck you. Remember, it is vital to diversify your investments.

Harnessing the Power of the Snowball Effect

Before looking at the concept of harnessing the power of the Snowball Effect, we must first understand the power of compound interest. Compound interest brings an interesting spin to the word "interest"; most people generally associate the word "interest" with debt; however, with compound interest, your interest works for you. Here's a simple definition: compound interest is the interest calculated on an initial investment or principal and on the accumulated interest in previous periods. Just think of it as an endless cycle of earning interest on previous interests you've accumulated. This results in your money growing at an exponential rate. For example, if you invest $100 and earn 10% interest, you will have $1,100. If you earn another 10% interest on that initial amount, you will have $1,210. This, my dear readers is the secret of every person on the Forbes 400. And this secret can also become yours if you decide to maintain a disciplined investment program.

How Compound Interest Works

Time is the secret ingredient in compound interest. It is vital to start early as the earlier you start, the more you save. In fact, an investment left untouched for a long timecan blossom into a huge amount in the future. With the following examples, let's look at how compound interest works. Barney, Alicia, and James all have access to the same 7% on their yearly investment return on their pension fund.

Barney starts investing at the age of 18. He invests $5,000 every year and stops 10 years later at 28 years old. The total sum of his investments stands at $50,000. When we factor in the power of compound interest on 7 percent yearly interest rate on his investments, Barney's total income is $602,070.

Alicia starts investing at the age of 28. She invests the same $5,000 every year until her retirement at 58 years old. Alicia has invested for 30 years and her investment stands at $150,000. When we factor in the power of compound interest on 7 percent yearly interest rate on her investments, Alicia's total income is $540,701.

Our next person is James, our most dedicated saver. James starts investing $5,000 yearly at age 18 and continues until he retires at 58 years old. Therefore, he has invested consistently for 40 years and his total investment stands at $200,000. When we factor in the power of compound interest on 7 percent yearly interest rate on his investments, James's total income is $1,142,811.

You're probably wondering this -why does Barney's account have a higher value than Alicia's? Alicia has invested three times the amount that Barney has. In fact, Alicia has saved for 30 years while Barney has only saved for 10. You see, that's the beauty of compound interest. This example shows the snowballing effect of the investment Barney made in the early years of his life. The snowball effect is so great that Alicia couldn't catch up, even if she had saved for another two decades.

In the above example, James is the perfect representation of consistent and early savings. Note the massive gap between his earnings and that of the other two - amazing, right? Compound investments favor those who start early and keep to it consistently.

Factors That Influence Compound Rates

There are many factors that could affect your compound returns. These factors determine how much compound interest you can accumulate during your set time frame.

Interest Rate

Your interest rate determines the rate of your snowball effect. This is the interest you earn on your investments, and on the profits you earn. If you are investing in stocks, this would affect your capital gains and dividends.

Tax Rate

The tax timing and tax rate payed to the government will determine the rate of your compound interest. Some investments come with little to no tax rate. For instance, 401[k], Traditional IRA, and some dividends stocks have this benefit. More so, you will end up with more income if you only pay your tax at the end of your investment period, instead of on a yearly basis.

Time

In the example above, time is the difference between James's earnings and the rest. The longer you grow your investment without any interruption, the faster your income snowballs to form a huge fortune. You can compare this principle to planting a tree. Naturally, a 30-year old tree will be bigger than when it was 10 years old.

Understanding the Time Value of Money in Compound Interests

This is a tricky but interesting concept that you need to understand about compound investment. A $100 bill a decade ago had more buying power than $100 in the present. The same amount in the present is more favorable than another of the same denomination in the future. This concept is referred to as the time value of money. It states that the value of money changes and depends on when a person is receiving it. Therefore, when you save your $100 by investing in a dividend-paying stock or any other investment, you are losing something called opportunity cost. Learning about the time value of money will help you to calculate compound interest. This will also help you to ask important questions like - If I need $1 million when I retire 40 years from now, and I can save $1,600 per month with 10% interest on my investment, will I reach my goal?

To get familiar with these concepts, you have to utilize a compound interest table, which shows you how your wealth can be affected by small changes over time. By taking a look at the compound table, you will see the influence of time and rate of interest on the general return. Once you get a hold of this concept, you will see that saving money alone doesn't guarantee you that million-dollar dream. For example, if you invest $10,000 in treasury bills, and earn 4% percent on the income for 50 years, you will end up with $71, 067 if you made the transaction through a tax-free account. If you invest the same amount in real estate and stock, with an average interest of 12 percent over the same time frame, you will earn upward of $2,890,022. You can see the gap between the returns on both investments. Thanks to a higher interest rate, the investor was able to utilize the power of compound interest.

	4%	8%	12%
10 years	$14,802	$21,589	$31,058
20 years	$21,911	$46,610	$96,463
30			

years	$32,434	$100,627	$299,600
40 years	$48,010	$217,245	$930,510
50 years	$71,067	$469,016	$$2,890,022

A Compound Table Showing the Value of $10,000 Invested With Varying Interest Rates

When you take a look at the compound interest table above, there's a clear difference between the compound interest of investments with 4% interest rate and those with a 12% percent interest rate. Most investors will often jump at the opportunity to invest with high interest rates in order to get the best returns in the future. However, chasing after investments with high interest rates is dangerous and you risk losing your investment along the way. It is probably the reason why Benjamin Graham, one of the world's foremost value investors, said that he lost a lot more chasing after a little more yield than to speculations in the stock market.

Immutable Dividend Strategies

Dividend investment offers the promise of a stable and continuous passive income. However, its promise of a safe and easy-to-use investment structure has ruined many unwary investors. Wait! Before you jump to conclusions, let me elaborate. It is so easy for people to let their guards down and ignore the risks involved in dividend investments. I'll tell you this: dividend investment is not child's play, even though it offers some of the safest ways of earning passive income. In fact, you need to arm yourself with proven strategies in order to navigate these waters. Mind you, just like every other strategy used in investments, these strategies are not infallible. However, you will get a fair chance to succeed using these strategies. So, let's get right to it!

Dogs of the Dow Strategy

Sounds fierce, right? Well, don't be fooled as this is one of the simplest dividend investment strategies. In fact, it's the ideal strategy for new investors. The Dogs of the Dow strategy focuses on stocks listed on the Dow Jones Industrial Average (DJIA). This begs the question: why is the Dow Jones so important? The Dow Jones Industrial Average (DJIA) is one of the oldest and most widely-recognized market indices in the world. Created by Charles Jones in the late 19th century, this index features 30 of the most influential and largest stocks in the NYSE and NASDAQ stock market. In fact, the Dow is often used as a measurement of the stock market.

The Dogs of the Dow strategy was brought to life by

Michael Higgins in 1991. Higgins based his research on the top 10 high dividend yield stocks and classified them as the investment dogs of the Dow Index. Today, this investment strategy has become both beginners and veteran investors' favorite. The strategy involves placing your money on 10 of the stocks with the highest dividend yields out of the 30 stocks in the Dow Index. Using this strategy, all the investor has to do is re-shuffle his investment portfolio so that his investments are spread equally across the 10 stocks.

Here's how it works: pick the 10 stocks with the highest dividend yield after the stock market closes on the last day of the year. Then, invest an equal amount into each of the selected stocks on the first day of the New Year. Hold the portfolio for a whole year and repeat the process for the year after. This time, you will calculate the total value of your portfolio, and divide the figure by 10. Let's say you arrived at 1,000 per stock. Furthermore, check to see if any of your current stocks are in the new list of high dividend-paying stocks. Sell off the stocks that didn't make the list and restore balance to your portfolio by investing in new stocks that made the list. So, how can you find the stocks with the highest dividend yield in this index? I have shown you how to calculate dividend yields in the previous chapters. Also, there are websites that feature the stocks in this sector with their dividends ratio.

Investors should practice caution when using this strategy. According to professional investors, investing in high yielding stocks doesn't necessarily mean they are undervalued; it could also be an indicator of financial distress and the removal of dividends in the future. Let's use the Eastman Kodak as an example of this theory. The company was a giant in the photography sector and a major constituent of the Dow Index. However, the company went bankrupt with the advent of digital photography. In addition to this, investors should not put a large fraction of their portfolio in a particular sector that pays high yields such as utilities. For this reason, there are now many variations of the Dow strategy, and it's important to consider these risks.

Variations of Dogs of the Dow Strategy

Many people have tried to modify this strategy to make it simpler and fool-proof. The variations include:

Small Dogs of the Dow

As usual, select the top 10 high-dividend paying stocks on the last day of the year. Out of these 10 dogs, pick the one that has the lowest stock prices. These are the small dogs. Invest an equal amount of cash in each of the selected stocks. Hold them for a year and repeat the whole process again. This variation is also called Dow 5.

Dow 4

This variation is similar to the previous one, except you pick 4 of the highest-dividend yield stocks.

Foolish 4

Created by the Motley Fool, this variation is similar to Dow 4. You pick the same stocks as Dow 4, allocate 40% of the portfolio to the lowest stock and put 20% of your portfolio in the other three.

Dividends Reinvestment Plan (DRIP)

We've already touched on this in dividend investments. So, I will gloss over the introduction and go straight to the main points. The dividend reinvestment plan is not a dividend strategy per se. Rather; it is a tool for long-term investments. The DRIP plan allows you to purchase additional shares by reinvesting your dividend payouts. You have to enroll for this plan before it can take effect in your portfolio. Once you enroll in it, you are no longer eligible to receive cash dividends. The cash is used to procure more shares.

Not all companies have offered the DRIP, but some big corporations like Wal-Mart, Procter and Gamble, and Abbvie Inc. have these plans. So, speak with your broker before you purchase the stocks. For your re-investment plan to take effect, you have to enroll in the DRIP prior to the record date. The DRIP is very lucrative and cheaper than buying stocks directly, as most companies offer a certain percentage of discount on stocks purchased via the DRIP. Here's another advantage of reinvesting through the DRIP - the price that you pay for the share is fixed from the average share price over a long time. This is better than paying for these shares directly.

One more thing I love about the Dividend Reinvestment plan is that you can decide to enroll fully or partially. I'll explain this shortly. Some investors are not patient enough to wait for years before they can see any returns on their investment, even if the plan will boost their returns in the future. Well, I'm not judging - different strokes for different folks. So, here's a way out for those who belong to the aforementioned category. You can decide to allocate a certain fraction of your shares into this plan. For example, if you hold 100 shares of Procter and Gamble (PG), you can decide to allocate 50 percent or 25 percent of the Dividend Reinvestment Plan. This means 50 or 25 percent of your dividends are reinvested in the plan. Furthermore, don't worry if you have already invested in a stock that doesn't have DRIP options. Some brokers offer DRIP alternative options like Charles Schwab, Armeritrade, and E*trade, to name a few.

Also, this plan is best suited for young investors since it enables them to harness the power of compound interest in their investment.

Moreover, you should know that allocating all or some of your shares in the DRIP doesn't exempt you from paying tax.

Dividend Exchange Traded Funds (ETF)

Dividend ETFs are a great avenue for investors with small capital. With the dividend ETF, investors are able to diversify their stocks without expending much income. Yes, the dividend exchange traded funds (ETF) is preferred over the common dividend stocks in some quarters. Many analysts in favor of dividend ETF cite the benefits of investing in a portfolio that spans across various sectors. What's more? With dividend ETFs, you can lower the commissions you pay to brokers for different shares from many dividend-paying companies. Another appealing benefit is that with this strategy, you don't have to worry about researching different types of company stocks; you simply have to invest and forget. Also, investors are able to invest in dividend ETFs with small capital without worrying about minimum deposit requirements and the performance of individual company stocks. In addition to this, the expense ratio is usually small for most ETFs, especially dividend ETFs, which are usually specific and apply to different scenarios.

For instance, high-yield ETFs focus on tracking high-paying dividend stocks while growth ETFs track the stocks of companies that are on the rise. The Vanguard Dividend Appreciation is an example of a growth ETF you can invest in. It has a 2.4 dividend yield.

There are also other types of ETFs that are just as exciting and interesting as dividend ETFs. For instance, IPO ETFs are great strategies for investors looking to take advantage of the potential upward growth of newly listed companies on the stock market. Investors in this niche are usually there for the short-term since the long-term success of these newly listed stocks are not guaranteed. On the other hand, we have the Index ETF to track established indexes like the S&P 500. You can buy and sell this ETF all day long on the stock exchange, and this also exposes you to different securities. Furthermore, index ETFs are not limited to tracking only domestic indexes, as you can also keep track of indexes in foreign markets. Lastly, we have the ETF of ETFs, which tracks other ETFs. Rather than invest in an underlying index, an ETF allows investors to invest in multiple and diverse indexes. It combines all the benefits of the traditional ETF structure. This strategy allows for more diversification as compared to other ETFs.

The Dividend Capture Strategy

Investments strategies have become hugely popular due to the fact that they promise more rewards than risks. The dividend capture strategy is one such strategy. Over time, this strategy has gained traction in usage since it offers a fool-proof way of earning more than 6 dividend payouts per year. Yes, it is a proven strategy. Before we get into the details of this strategy, let's first define it.

What is Dividend Capture Strategy?

The dividend capture strategy is a time-driven strategy that involves the buying and selling of dividend-paying stocks. This strategy takes advantage of the loophole of buying a stock just before the ex-dividend date to capture the dividends, and holding on to it till the dividends are paid. To refresh your mind, the ex-dividend date is the day you are entitled to receive dividends on your stocks. It comes after the declaration date, in which companies announce the date and amount of dividends to be paid. After this comes the record date, the pay date when companies determine which shareholders are eligible to receive dividends, and the date when the dividends are actually paid.

Getting back on topic, investors take advantage of the financial rule that states that investors are eligible to receive dividends from a company even if they hold the stocks for one day. This strategy is a contrast to traditional investment approaches that focus on buying and holding stocks long enough to gain profit and harness the snowball effect. Investors who use this strategy often chase after high yield dividend stocks, since the strategy becomes profitable with high dividends.

How It Works

The dividend capture strategy's appeal lies in its simplicity and ease of transaction. You don't have to spend long hours studying different investment portfolios or charts. All you have to do is purchase the stock before the ex-dividend date and sell the shares on or after the ex-dividend date, as investors don't have to wait for dividends before selling off the stock. Sometimes, an investor might have to wait for the share price to bounce back to its original value if the price falls after the dividend announcements.

As mentioned earlier, the Dividend Capture Strategy is a loophole in the market. In fact, it's a testament to the fact that the market doesn't conform to perfect logic. If the market was perfect, we would see a reflection of the dividend amount in the stocks' prices until the ex-dividend date. However, the stock market doesn't work that way - an investor is often able to recoup a substantial fraction of the dividends despite selling off the stock at a slight loss following the ex-dividend date. Let's look at a real-life scenario to understand this better.

Real-Life Example

On July 11, 2011, the stock price of Coca-Cola on the market was $66.52. The following day, the board of directors at Coca-Cola announced the quarterly dividend payment of $0.35 and that the stock price increased to $66.87. Well, that is the stock price in theory, but the price might be lower considering the market volatility. Six weeks after the announcement date, the stock was trading at a lower price of $64.94. This is the time when the dividend capture investor would purchase the company stocks. The following day, the dividends were declared, and the stock prices rose up to 65.84. This is the perfect time for the investor to sell off the stocks and receive both the dividends and capital gain. However, this plan only looks good on paper because there are several factors that might affect the outcome of this strategy in the equity market.

Shortcomings of Dividend Capture

Some dividend payouts attract different tax percentages, depending on the investor's taxable income. Most times, the dividends collected via this strategy often fail to meet the necessary requirements to receive favorable tax conditions. Therefore, the investor is taxed at the rate of an ordinary income tax. According to tax agencies like the IRS, you must hold the stocks for no less than 60 days prior to an ex-dividend date, before you can receive favorable tax rates on your investment. Hold on! Don't lose hope. There's a way to get around this clause. The way to do so is to purchase a stock just a day before its ex-dividend date and hold it for 61 days before selling. You will qualify for the 60-day favorable tax rate if you employ this method. After the sell, you can reinvest the money into another company to start the trend again. In addition to this, if you try the 60-day holding period, you will effectively earn six dividend payments per year, as opposed to quarterly dividend payments.

Finally, some companies might not pay dividends, which may affect the success of this strategy. In fact, some companies might prefer to reinvest their earnings into the company instead of paying out dividends.

How to Build Your Dividend Portfolio

Imagine having an ice cream stand that sells ice cream, and nothing else. You always make great sales on sunny days, especially in summer, but not so much in winter and in rainy weather, a period where you make little to no sales. However, if you sold umbrellas and hot coffee beverages along with your ice cream business, you would probably make great sales, irrespective of the weather. In fact, you would have a stable income since you would never shut down, regardless of the weather. And that, my dear reader, is the reason why you need to diversify your investment portfolio. The main reason for this is to generate a continuous stream of passive income irrespective of the market conditions. In the previous chapter, we have already covered the reasons why you need to diversify. In this section, we will take a look at the ways in which you can build your dividend portfolio to withstand the volatility of the stock market.

Building a Diversified Global Portfolio

This is where I talk about the "home bias." Many investors are reluctant to step outside their comfort zone, which in this case, is the global stock market. For instance, about 90 percent of the average US investor's stocks are held in the local global market. Despite the fact that the US stock market represents a small percentage of the world's market value, these investors often prefer to play it safe with the local market. We could understand the "home bias" in the past since there was no international exchange to trade funds. However, the world is now increasingly connected and there's no better time to take advantage of a global diversified portfolio than now. I'm not saying you should jump into unfamiliar stocks in a bid to diversify. It is not an excuse to be careless.

So, here are a few questions to ask yourself to know if your portfolio contains the right mix of diversified stocks.

How many investments should you have?

In truth, there's no official or set number of investments that you should hold. However, you are inviting disaster if you need both hands to count your investments. When you have that much investment, there are chances that you have stocks that overlap or are in arcane sectors. The truth is, you don't have to stick your hands in so many individual stocks. All you have to do to cover both international and domestic stock is to invest in 3 main index funds; a total international stock fund, a total US bond market fund and a total US stock market fund. Mind you, you can also invest in smaller market ETFs or indexes. The main point is to avoid investing in stocks that overlap and not to have too many investments in your portfolio.

Do you really understand your investments?

In the rules of dividend investments, I emphasized the point of never investing in any stock that you don't understand and can't explain to a layman. This is a question you ought to often ask yourself. I'm not talking about knowing the figures or percentages of what an investment will bring. This is about knowing how those figures that you easily quote, are calculated. If you don't understand how an investment works, then you can't be sure you really need it.

Can you explain why you bought each stock?

I'm not talking about flimsy explanations such as; I bought it because it was mentioned in a TV program or because it was listed in some article on a random website. No! That is not an acceptable answer. Aside from knowing how an investment works, you need to understand the specific role an investment has in your portfolio. What's more? You should be able to quantify the benefits you receive from owning an investment by referring to performance figures that show how it leans more towards returns than risks.

Do you still have some investment touched after buying?

It is easy to leave some investment untouched because they bring in some high returns. Let's say you have a long-term investment strategy and you have tailored your portfolio to tally with your financial goals. Your portfolio might contain 40 percent bond stocks, 10 percent small company stocks, and 50 percent large company stocks. This combination or any other you deem fit to integrate should reflect your risk tolerance and your financial goals. Since you earn varying returns from different investments, you should learn how to balance your portfolio and restore it to your original combination. You can sell from shares from the winning stocks, and invest them into the laggards, in order to bring balance to your portfolio.

Do you frequently add new investments to your portfolio?

You are courting danger if you frequently add new investments to your portfolio. The aim of earning passive income is to find a rhythm or balance that works for you. Once you find that rhythm or a balanced portfolio, your work as an investor is done. Surely, there is some monitoring, balancing, and the occasional buying and selling of stocks that is necessary. However, you don't need to consistently add new stocks or assets as consistently as investment firms bring them out. Doing so, you will end up with a mish-mash of imbalanced investments that you don't know how to handle.

Robinhood Trading Software as an Effective Tool to Build Your Dividend Portfolio

The Robinhood trading software generated a lot of attention and outcry from brokers and the general public. This company based their whole campaign on the abolition of brokerage fee and zero percent commissions. Most online brokers generally charge commission fees between $1 and $7 per transaction. Robinhood, on the other hand, claims brokers are ripping off investors. Therefore, they don't charge a dime. More so, it enables investors to invest in dividend-paying stocks, without the clutter of complex research and information on the stock market. To help you understand how to use this software, I have created a list of things to know about Robinhood - think of it as a crash course.

What You Need To Know Before Investing in Robinhood

There are no commissions on US stocks

Yes, it's completely free for US-commissioned stocks. This is a great avenue for investors with little capital and minimal experience to earn passive income from their stocks. With this app, you don't need to wait until you have enough capital to buy enough shares of your favorite stock. You can buy as low as one share of a stock. For instance, about 76 shares of Hewlett-Packard are worth $10.75, so you can buy one share for $0.14. You can also go for a single share of high-yield dividend stocks of tech companies like Google at $890. However, you will still be charged a trading activity fee if you decide to sell off your stock, but this amount is minimal and less than most fees charged by online brokers.

There is no dividend re-investment package

Unfortunately, Robinhood doesn't offer this service yet, as all your dividend payouts are credited as cash into your account. However, through the computer share account, some dividends earned from stocks such as Clorox (CLX) are reinvested to purchase new stocks. Another downside of not getting to reinvest your dividends is that you have to wait until you have earned enough dividends to buy the stock you want. For instance, if you earned $30 in dividends this month and you wanted to reinvest in a stock that's worth $120, you would have to wait until you'd have enough funds to purchase it.

Limited Investment Options

Robinhood doesn't come with a lot of options. Those looking to diversify their portfolios beyond dividend-bearing stocks are bound to be disappointed. So, Robinhood is not for those looking to invest in foreign stocks or trade options. Furthermore, Robinhood does not have a platform for trading index funds yet. However, you can compensate for this setback by putting part of your cash into investment accounts with these options.

You can also attend shareholder meetings.

This is something most investors don't get to do with other investment platforms. You have a voice when you officially become a shareholder on this platform. Sometimes, the platform sends notifications to alert you of an impending meeting. However, some investors miss out on these meetings due to different time zones.

Don't Fall For The Hype!

It is easy to get lost and distracted when using the Robinhood App. When you open this app, there are usually lots of news alerts and notifications. Some of these news alerts show different headlines from different financial sites, and it's easy to get distracted. Remember that it is easy to make wrong trading decisions when you get distracted. So, learn to keep your emotions in check when you next open this app.

There are no monthly plans

Robinhood doesn't have a function that will enable you to automate your investments. Automated investments are a great way of keeping your investment on track, as you don't have to worry about spending time on investing your monthly or yearly income quota into your portfolio. Investors on this platform will stay up-to-date with their monthly purchase, even if they have to take the time and stress to log into this software.

Automatic Deposits

Robinhood investors don't have the option of automated investment plans. They can, however, set up the option of automated deposits from their bank to their Robinhood account. In addition to this, users can set up automatic deposits as per their requirements, from weekly, monthly, to yearly deposits. With Robinhood's flexible deposit rate, you can finally have more control over how much you invest.

No minimum amount

You definitely have no excuse for not investing. Unlike normal investment accounts where you are required to have upwards of $1,000, all you need is to have enough funds to purchase the shares you want to buy. When you combine the zero commission rates with no minimum deposit, you will see that this software is an ideal tool for those with limited funds.

It is faster to purchase stocks with Robinhood

It's not surprising that Robinhood has a huge appeal with millennials and the younger generation. In fact, I would say it takes less than 30 seconds to purchase the stock you want. You don't have to worry about longwaiting periods before making a purchase. Additionally, you will get a confirmation e-mail immediately as you buy shares.

In recent years, Robinhood has become an indispensable tool for dividend investments. However, this software comes with setbacks that might jeopardize your earnings and investments.

Mistakes You Ought To Avoid with Robinhood

When dealing with an unfamiliar platform such as Robinhood, it's normal to make some mistakes. Therefore, I have a created a list of mistakes you need to avoid on this app.

Never buy in real-time

This is a rookie mistake. Most new users don't know that there are different ways of buying stock on this platform. The real-time is the default option for buying stocks. When buying stocks in real-time, it is often impossible to get the exact price you want due to the delay in the process. To access the other type of options that you want, click on the stock you want, tap "Buy," and proceed to the top left corner and click on "orders." The options in "Orders" are: Stop Limit Order, Limit Order, and Stop Loss. For instance, you can dictate the price at which you want to buy the shares by clicking on the "Limit Order." So, when the stock price gets to that point, the system will automatically purchase it for you.

Add Money In Advance

It takes about 3 days to transfer your money from your bank account to Robinhood. During this waiting period, a lot of changes and favorable deals would have taken place. It is a painful experience not to have the funds to purchase the stocks that you desire. So, always make sure you have enough funds in case you come across a stock you want to buy.

Don't Check Your Stocks Every Day

Do you want to die of worry? If you do, check your stock price every time you have a free moment! This is the equivalent of checking your weight every time you've had a heavy meal or a long exercise. You should know that fluctuations are normal in the stock market. So, don't get freaked out by these little changes. Better still; track your stocks every month by using a spreadsheet. This is advisable if you are holding these stocks for a whole year. You will gain more perspective over your market trend by doing so. So, don't fall prey to your emotions, and don't start selling off your stocks at the slight drop of a pin. What's more? You can follow Yahoo stocks, Google News, and any other stock analytics website to get a feel for stock market events.

Don't Rely on Robinhood For All Your Research!

There are websites out there that'll give you an in-depth analysis of stock growth and performance. Robinhood should not be your only source for stock news, as the stock prices indicated only go back one year. On websites like Yahoo Stocks, you can see stock prices for the last 10 years, or even longer. Furthermore, Wikiwealth is an ideal source for recommendations of stocks based on Warren Buffet's selections. It will also show you a company's cash flow and possible returns. ClosingBell, on the other hand, is an efficient alert system. It compiles user ratings and analyst views. You can integrate ClosingBell into your Robinhood app.

Conclusion

Finally, we've now reached the end of this short book. After writing on the essence and mechanics of dividends and investments as a whole, one thing that sticks to my mind is the beauty of breaking free from the rat race of a rigid income, without making much impact. Investments give you the ability to decide how your life will turn out to be. It is beyond the circumstances of birth, race or social class! Your dream of becoming what you want to become is at the other side of investments. Warren Buffet only had a million dollars worth of stocks in 1962. Today, he is one of the wealthiest men alive. You might not have a million dollar of stocks in your portfolio. Heck, you might not even have up to $1,000. The important thing is to keep your eyes fixated on the dream and work towards achieving it by harnessing the power of compound interests and investments. Mind you, I am not saying you will become rich overnight. Keep dreaming, and never let your dreams fade away. And remember, don't procrastinate - start early! As a matter of fact, start now!